DATE DUE

JAN 20			
NOV 18			
NOV 10			
MAY 9			
Speckman			

Eating and Cooking Around the World

Most of us eat with our fingers — sometimes. What better way to eat corn-on-the-cob, or watermelon, or a drumstick? And would picnics be half as much fun if we had to eat with knives and forks? However, we only eat with our fingers once in a while — generally it is considered more polite to eat meals at a table with a full set of silverware.

But eating and cooking vary as much as do languages, and for just as good reasons. In *Eating and Cooking Around the World* Erick Berry not only pictures the remarkably different ways in which people prepare their meals and eat them, but also explains how different conditions in each country have dictated these strange customs. Through text and pictures we tour the places where people eat with their fingers; we visit the Eskimos, who have little but meat and fish to live on, and the islands of the Caribbean, where people are almost wholly vegetarian, as well as the chopstick countries where rice is the main dish.

EATING AND COOKING
AROUND THE WORLD

Fingers Before Forks

Erick Berry

ILLUSTRATED

The John Day Company   New York   56797

For Ann Gannon
who started it all.

Library of Congress Catalog Card Number: 63-10227

Manufactured in the United States of America

0100-0140

CONTENTS

FOREWORD

It is an old saying that "Fingers were made before forks." For thousands of years our ancestors ate only with their fingers, just as some animals, such as raccoons, eat today — neatly — with their front paws. Then men began using their hunting knives to hack meat from bones and convey it to their mouths. The next invention was the spoon, to deal with liquid stews. This may have been a small gourd cut in half, part of a sea shell or a coconut shell. Forks were not invented until sometime in the Middle Ages, and are said to have come to England by way of Italy. A lady carried her own personal fork; for a long time a man did not bother with anything so fussy; he preferred to keep on eating with his knife and fingers.

But there are millions of people in the world today who do not use the fork at all. They still eat with their fingers, and very tidily too. Or they use chopsticks, which are a sort of extension of the fingers of one hand. Both these ways of eating are good manners in their own countries.

Table manners around the world can tell us a good deal about what foods people live on in different countries and how they cook those foods. And eating is one of the three or four habits common to all humans.

One of the simplest and clearest ways to group people, regardless of whether they use fingers or forks, is by calling them hunters, herdsmen and farmers.

The hunter cannot develop a very organized tribal life as he needs much land to rove in. A hunter becomes a herdsman when he begins to keep his animals for breeding, and feeding them himself instead of killing them for food when he catches them. Hunters may also forage; they pick wild berries, nuts and fruits where they find them. Herders, too, have to forage for this addition to their diets. But when they begin to plant such things near home, and gather and store them season after season, then the herders become farmers.

This pattern is true all down through the history of man. We have all three of these groups existing today around the world, and all three are steps toward what we call civilization—a word which means "city dweller."

We will begin the story of eating and cooking around the world with the first of the three groups, the hunters. In the first two chapters we will meet hunters in very different parts of the world — the far north and the tropics. Through the story of the Lapps, we will see how hunters develop into herders. Then we will meet more herdsmen — Arab herdsmen of the desert. Finally, we will be introduced to the farmers. We will be taken to the countries of farmers all over the world from the Americas to Africa and Asia.

ESKIMO COUNTRY

ALASKA · ARCTIC OCEAN · GREENLAND · ARCTIC · CIRCLE · NORTHWEST TERRITORIES OF CANADA.

HUNTERS OF THE FAR NORTH

Long before our ancestors penned in cattle and bred their own animals, before they plowed the land and made farms, they lived entirely by hunting. There are not many people in the world today who eat only the meat they kill for themselves. Most of the markets depend on herds of cattle, sheep and other animals raised especially for sale, and on farms which grow fruits and vegetables especially for the table. But there are still some parts of the world where diets are limited through necessity: deserts, where there is too little water to raise crops; and far-northern places, where the summers are too short and the ground too deeply frozen for the inhabitants to depend on what they can tame or what they can grow.

Among such people are the Eskimos living on the

most northern tip of North America. The Eskimo lives there because no one has ever wanted to take the land away from him; not even the early Indians could exist in a country so desolate and dangerous.

It is a wide stretch of country, extending from northern Alaska eastward through Labrador to Greenland. The various tribes of Eskimos are related, but each tribe has its own kind of hunting. One hunts the caribou; another tribe hunts the wild mountain sheep; still another lives on the meat of the forest moose. The tribes that live along the shore depend on what they can harpoon from the sea; walrus, seal and some kinds of whale, and what fish they can catch in their nets and traps or with spears.

The caribou, which is a cousin of the reindeer but slightly larger and much wilder, can find little food in this barren land. They must stay close together in herds, to protect each other from their great enemy the wolf. Each year large herds of caribou migrate, traveling northward in search of summer grazing, then southward again for the winter as the northern land grows cold and dark.

If this stream of countless caribou — a brown torrent of moving animals — passes near an Eskimo village, the hunters can kill more meat than they can use at one time. Luckily, so far north, they can just let it freeze, and so preserve it for future use.

The Eskimos of whom we hear most, those tribes living along the Arctic Ocean, have quite a different source of food, and so have developed a different type of hunting. When the sea is frozen, the hunter of the family, usually the father, grandfather or eldest son, harpoons seal, narwhale or walrus, through holes he has cut in the heavy ice, or through airholes as the creatures come up to breathe. When the seas are more open, the hunter paddles out in his kayak, a sealskin canoe. He can even harpoon whales from

Eskimos eating meat in an igloo. Caribou-fat lamp and drying rack.

this light craft. This is a very dangerous way of finding food.

All these methods of hunting give the Eskimo only a fish or meat diet. He must have vegetables of some kind. Like all hunting tribes, he has learned to forage — that is, to collect what nature has provided in the wild state. Inland he will collect edible mosses, lichens and berries; he will look for the nests of wild birds for eggs. In April the Eskimo makes his salad from the undigested greenery, usually reindeer moss, in the stomach of the caribou he slays. And along the coast his greatest delicacies are the half-digested clams from the stomach of the walrus he has captured. Like the African lion, which usually eats first the contents of the stomach of his prey, the primitive hunter instinctively knows what is best for him, without science having to tell him.

In some parts of this cold country a wild fowl, called the eider duck, is eaten raw. The auk, a large sea bird, is given special treatment for the Eskimo table. The birds are packed tight, feathers and all, into a sealskin bag which still has the seal blubber or fat inside the skin. As this freezes and thaws, the meat is softened and the seal oil gradually penetrates the birds, pickling them, like sardines in olive oil. When they are taken out to eat, the feathers pull away easily and the meat is as tender as though it had been cooked.

These, then, are the Eskimo hunter's sources of food. Let us see what he does with these foods.

Caribou and Seal Blubber

The word "Eskimo" means "Eaters of Raw Meat," and this is generally true of his diet. White explorers in the Arctic have had little difficulty living on uncooked food. They tell us that a lump of blubber, half frozen, may taste as good as the best candy, because the mouth knows what the body needs. In this icy climate, fats and oils are very important in the diet; the body burns them up, the way a furnace burns up heating fuel.

During the long months of the winter, when the seashore tribes live in the igloo, they have an unusual problem in cooking. The dome-shaped kitchen, which is also sleeping and living room, is made of carefully cut snow blocks, and is almost airtight. For the sake of greater warmth, there is only one low-built passageway for entrance. Wood is too precious to burn, and anyway the Eskimo needs whatever driftwood he can find, for making harpoons and sleds. Also, a wood fire would find no outlet for smoke. Long before anyone else in the world, he learned to cook and heat by using oil. He invented a saucer-shaped bowl, flat on one side, carved from soapstone. This is his "stove."

Into this bowl, called a *kudlik,* the housewife places the blubber fat of the seal, mashed into small bits. Or it is hung in a narrow strip over the already lighted lamp. The melting fat seeps down into the bowl, where it begins to burn. The wick is made of dried moss, plaited with a cottonlike wild plant. It burns with a hot, smokeless flame. Over this tiny fire the housewife sets up a frame made of barrel staves or of bone, crisscrossed with sealskin thongs, and supported by sticks thrust into the ground. This odd arrangement forms a

13

drying frame for mittens, boots and socks. It is also the cook fire. Here, in an iron pot, the stew is cooked, for stew is the Eskimo's main dish. Since he has no cereal of any kind, there is no bread.

Eskimo housekeeping could hardly exist without the deep-freeze. Yes, really a deepfreeze. Did you know that we learned about quick freezing from these hunters of the far North?

For many generations, humans have preserved food by chilling it. They have even frozen it. Then a man named Birdseye, on a trip to the far North, discovered that food frozen very rapidly, in extreme cold, tasted far better when it was thawed out than food that had been frozen more slowly. You can imagine how important this method of preserving fish and meat has always been to the Eskimo, for he may kill twenty caribou in a single week, and then see no more for months to come, or if he lives on the seashore and kills a whale, he may need this supply for his family and sled dogs for many weeks. What makes this quick-freezing still more important is that the Eskimo has no foods that he can store easily, like beans, corn and grain, such as more southern folk gather, to hoard and use for one or two seasons, until the next good harvest.

Also, these people are nomads, often forced to follow game wherever it goes. Nomads cannot afford to carry much weight, extra stores of food, cookpots and eating tools. They must eat picnic fashion all the year around.

There is no special mealtime in the Eskimo household. The Eskimo eats when he is hungry, stuffing himself against a probable period of starvation ahead. The men are first to gather around the stewpot, dipping their fingers in, to pick

14

out the tastiest pieces of meat. The eater pops one end of the large lump into his mouth, then *flip, flip,* his knife cuts off the rest of the lump close to his lips, and so on, mouthful by mouthful, to the end of the morsel. The man's knife is also his hunting knife, which is much like the one we know. But the woman uses a different kind of cutting tool, shaped like a half-moon or the chopper used in a chopping bowl. It is called a *ulu.* This was originally the shoulder blade of a seal, walrus or caribou, sharpened and shaped to a cutting edge. Nowadays it is made of steel.

It is only when the men of the household have fed that the women and children can eat. This is not bad manners; it is a custom among all hunting people. If the head of the household should weaken for lack of food . . . and food is very hard to get . . . he will be unable to kill more game, and the whole family will starve. Each member of the family has to be rationed according to his usefulness. Thus the first choice of food begins with the hunter himself and runs down through the scale to the women and children — then the old and helpless, who come last.

Much of the Eskimo's food is eaten raw. Big slabs of blubber and of meat, and bags of frozen blood, hang outside the hut, high up and well out of reach of the sled dogs or of wolves. A hunter passing this store will hack off a piece with his hunting knife, much as you might help yourself to food from the refrigerator.

Nowadays most families own a kerosene stove. And if they live within reach of a trade store, they purchase many additional groceries there; sugar, flour, dried milk, coffee and tea. Tea is preferred to coffee, as being lighter to carry, and is one of the Eskimo's greatest luxuries. When the stove is not

The Eskimo woman cuts off the meat, close to her lips, with the *ulu.*

being used for stewing, the teakettle is constantly on the boil. Everyone wants tea, quantities of it, hot and extremely strong. When it has brewed for a long time, a little snow is added to cool it, and guests and host dip in their enameled mugs, drinking till there is nothing left but the tea leaves in the bottom. Then everyone reaches in eager fingers, to dip those leaves out and eat them also.

Today many Eskimos live much as we do, following the diet and eating habits of the Americans and Canadians around them. They live in wooden houses much like ours, and work as skilled mechanics on planes and in airports. But many still follow the old ways, and it is of those we have told you here.

THE ISLAND FISHERMEN

Now we travel a long way, half around the world, to a people who once lived almost entirely on fish. Most fisherfolk are still in the "hunting" stage. They seek out their game. They follow it, whether by ocean or river. They lie in wait in a canoe, with hook and line, or net or spear. They put down traps; they spear fish in the shallows. All very much as a hunter seeks his game in the forest.

We now come to the Hawaiian Islands. The early Hawaiians knew more than six hundred kinds of fish. Many of these, even today, are still called by their Hawaiian names.

Just as hunters started to herd and breed animals, so, in a few cases, these fish hunters began to fence in and breed fish. In Hawaii, the fish were raised in special ponds — the favorite fish being the mullet. They were first caught in traps or nets with other fish, then the others were weeded out and the chosen species fed and encouraged to breed.

You can easily see the advantage of this practice. Just as the early herdsmen provided against a scarcity of wild game and a bad season by taming his animals, so the Hawaiian fishermen provided against a possible change in the migration route of fish, or against prolonged storms that would make it impossible to launch their frail boats.

Still another race had made a step forward in history from an uncertain hand-to-mouth existence to one that provided more security for the future.

Fish Farms and Feasts

The Hawaiian Islands were first settled by people who came north from Samoa, a long way south in the Pacific Ocean. These people were called Polynesians, from *polynesia*, a word that means "many islands." They are believed to have made this 2,000-mile voyage, a long one for their frail, open boats, about 500 B.C.

These early settlers brought with them not only the food for their dangerous voyage but living beasts, and plants from which they planned to grow their future food. The plants were taro roots, banana and breadfruit shoots, coconut and sugarcane. Since livestock on such a long voyage would be hard to keep alive in an open canoe and difficult to feed, the

Pounding *poi* in Hawaii. A man can consume eighteen pounds of poi a day.

animals were few and carefully chosen. Two hens and a cock, two bitches and a dog — for they ate dogs then — and two sows, with a boar pig. These early people must have had great self-control not to eat any of these valuable supplies when they grew hungry; just as our early American pioneers must have had, to preserve enough seed and breeding stock during their first hungry years. And as our pioneers lived on wild game until their first crops were harvested, so those early immigrants to the islands must have lived wholly on fish until their plants and livestock had begun to multiply. This may have been the start of their "fish farms."

One method of saving these essential foodstuffs seems to have been something called a *tabu*. This Polynesian word means "forbidden," and has now become a label for similar customs all over the world. A powerful chief or a religious leader issues an order that something must *not* be done, or must *not* be eaten. The penalty for breaking tabu was a religious punishment, bringing ill luck and often death.

For instance, there were certain foods tabu to women. This tabu, like an all-seeing, ghostly policeman, stalked the islands, making sure that women did not touch pork, coconuts, or certain kinds of fish. Right up to modern times, women could not eat with men, and food for men and women must not even be cooked in the same oven.

Hence the early Hawaiian man of the house was also the cook of the house, since the preparation of *poi*, the staple diet, was wholly his job. He consumed as much as eighteen pounds of this in a day — a heavy burden to prepare. One rather wonders what the women did with their spare time!

It is probable that some of these tabus were intended to preserve from the women such essential staples as pig and coconut during the time when the men were absent on long voyages and could not keep an eye on them. There is usually a sensible reason for primitive native customs.

Poi must have been important from the very early days, for the first settlers brought with them their poi-pounders — heavy, squat stone pestles. And after more than a thousand years, poi is still the main "bread" of the islands, which produce no grain or cereal, and for a long time probably had no yams or sweet potatoes. The all-important basis of poi is the taro, a lilylike plant with long, heart-shaped leaves and a starchy root. It grows in swampy places. The leaves may be cooked as greens, as we cook spinach, but need thorough and prolonged boiling to rid them of poisonous juices. The roots are roasted and steamed, then peeled and pounded with the stone pestle, in a wooden mortar. It is heavy work and a task which was once only undertaken by the men.

During this pounding, water is slowly added till a dough-like mass is produced. This dough, or poi, is wrapped in green leaves, and will keep for weeks. It is this food that made the long Polynesian voyages possible. For eating, water is added. It would seem flavorless to us, but its slightly acid taste is much appreciated by the islanders. Additional relish is gained by flavoring it with any one of some forty kinds of seaweed and algae, steeped into a vitamin-rich sauce.

Poi was also made from sweet potatoes and from breadfruit, by much the same process. Nowadays most of this work is done in a poi factory, where the root is cleaned, washed, and run through a machine. It is certainly a lot easier than in the old days, but something fundamental has been lost from the life of the people.

22

Today the Hawaiian oven, the *imu,* in which taro is baked, is little altered, however. It is a mere trench in the ground, with no shelter over it. Kindling wood is placed in this trench, then larger and larger pieces of wood are added, and the fire lighted. On top of all this, arches made of special imu stones are arranged. These stones have special heating properties and are saved from one fire to another; some of them are very old. Finally, layers of breadfruit, taro and sweet potato are packed in, covered with mats and sacks that have been well soaked in water, and the whole left to steam. Taro takes from three to four hours to cook in this imu oven.

Chicken and pig are much used in today's island diet. Fish, of course, is popular and is prepared in a number of ways. It may be wrapped in *ti* leaves (a ti is a kind of palm tree) and steamed in the imu with the vegetables; or it may be boiled in a calabash (a bottle-shaped gourd) into which hot stones are dropped. Unlike the Japanese, the Hawaiians did not eat raw fish, even in the old days. When there was a surplus, it was either salted or dried, to preserve it. For this drying process, there is more sunshine in Hawaii than in Japan.

In the early days the women did not sit down to a big daily dinner with the men; they ate cold snacks out of baskets as they went about their daily tasks. But a great feast included everyone. Even today, any excuse will serve for a feast — a homecoming, a birth, a victory in sports, a big haul of fish; in the early days victory in battle was celebrated by feasting. Such a feast is called a *luau;* this means "leaf of the taro plant," perhaps because it is on this leaf, so large and tough, that the food is served. Banana leaves are also used as platters or plates.

Swiftly and skillfully, the pig is lowered into the *imu* oven.

Wherever you go on the islands, the center of the feast — the very king of the luau — is the pig. A good luau pig may weigh between 150 and 300 pounds on the hoof, and you can see that it takes plenty of muscle as well as skill to prepare this monster dish. In the outer islands, which are less influenced today by the tourist, the feast begins when the whole family, friends and neighbors, drop in to watch, to chat and to advise.

For a party of sixty, the dressed pig should weigh about 90 pounds. While the imu stones are heating, the whole hog is being prepared nearby. The insides are removed, the knuckles skinned, and bristle carefully shaved off. Rock salt and soybean sauce are rubbed into the meat, inside and out. When this is well soaked in, the pig is ready for the hot imu stones to be shoveled into its stomach and shoulder cavities. Steam rises and flames shoot up as the seared pork catches fire, but the flames are beaten out with ti leaves. The pig's front and back legs are tied together, and it is lifted to rest on a screen of wire mesh.

The imu has been carefully lined with several inches of broad, green banana leaves, which will keep the meat moist as it cooks, and help to flavor it. Quickly the men hoist the prize from the table over to the pit, and at the last minute, yams, bananas and whole fish, wrapped in ti leaves, are tucked around the meat, to cook slowly. Dripping-wet burlap bags are spread over the oven; in the old days homemade tapa cloth, woven from the bark of a kind of mulberry tree, was used for this. Then earth is shoveled on top until all is completely covered.

The imu must be carefully watched for escaping steam. The men stay with it hour after hour, all day long, to heap on

25

more earth when such steam vents appear. At the end of the day, when the hour for the feast draws nearer, there is much excitement as layers of the steaming earth are shoveled away. The roasted pig is lifted from the pit to a table, and buckets of cold water await the cooks. To remove the hot stones, the men plunge their hands into the water, grab the rocks from inside of the pig, and toss them out. Dip, grab, toss; dip, grab, toss. The secret of it is skill and speed. At last the fragrant aroma of roast pork reaches the nostrils. There is nothing quite like it, and the flavor of the succulent meat is beyond compare.

It would be difficult to find any people who derive more pleasure from eating than the Hawaiians. The luau feast is still, as in the old days, a symbol of hospitality and of the art of good living.

Polynesian Poi and Pork

Samoa, over 2,000 miles southwest of Hawaii, was the earlier home of the Hawaiians, the island from which they sailed so many centuries ago. From Samoa, the Hawaiians took many of their traditions with regard to food and eating, but over the centuries there have been many changes in these. It is interesting to go back to the earlier race, and compare the two sets of customs.

For instance, in Samoa, as in Hawaii, the heavy cooking is still done by the men. This may explain why the Samoans have only one cookday a week, and no dishes to wash. Fish is the main, everyday diet, and there are the usual breadfruit,

Samoa. After the grown-ups have eaten, the children dine on leftovers.

chicken, coconuts and bananas, but, as in Hawaii, pork is the main dish for feasts.

Very early on a Friday morning — even before the sun rises or they have eaten — the men take their long canoes out to the fishing grounds. While they are gone, the women round up the pigs that will be needed for that week's feast, slay and prepare them. The women also fetch firewood and the necessary banana leaves. In midmorning the triumphant fleet returns with the catch, and the villagers troop down to welcome it on the beach. Ceremonial *kava* is served in coconut shells, and the catch is brought up to the big, outdoor oven.

27

The imu is used much as it is in Hawaii, only in Samoa the oven is all above ground, not in a trench. The trench, which is surely more effective, seems to have been the invention of some bright Hawaiian cook, after the people left Samoa. This Samoan imu is always in the same spot, but here the cooking is not done all at one time, as in Hawaii. The oven is kept heated for only an hour or two, since this is to be only the first roasting of several. And for this reason the breadfruit must be not quite ripe, the bananas must be green, and the pork, when taken out of the oven, should be nearly raw. That's how the Samoans like it.

In the dining room of the long, many-pillared communal house each man, head of his family, has his appointed seat on the ground before his own special pillar. Food is served on large, wooden platters kept for this purpose, and is brought in by the young maids and youths of the village. Water, the main drink, is served in coconut shells, and the food is picked up with the fingers. For the softer portions, the eater may use a piece of leaf as a scoop or spoon.

The odd thing about this weekly meal is that the very large portions served on each platter are not intended to be eaten at one sitting, or even by one person. Behind each householder sits another male member of his family. It is his task to receive and store away in a basket the portions that are passed back to him from the large platter. This custom applies only to flesh foods; chicken and pork. It does not apply to fish, since recooked seafoods are liable to be poisonous in a hot climate. You can see, also, that this is another way for the head of the family to get the best portions, since he is the breadwinner and the hunter, as was the Eskimo in our earlier chapter.

Guests do not wait for all to finish the meal. When they have eaten, they call for bowls of water in which to wash their hands; then take their departure. The young people will eat later, at the back of the communal hall.

Such food as is taken home to the huts may last the family all that week. It will be recooked and supplemented by fruits, fish and vegetables, and of course the universal poi, for the single large meal of each day. As in Hawaii, the women working in the fields carry little baskets of food from which they eat small snacks from time to time. It is an easy life for the women. And if the weather is favorable for fishing, not a difficult life for the men, since it is only once a week that they have to prepare that large meal.

The ceremonial drink of the Samoans is unusual. It is called *kava*. It is mildly intoxicating, though not alcoholic; for those not accustomed to the drink, it produces sleepiness and a feeling of melancholy. But in Samoa it is considered of great importance, and no ceremony is complete without it.

Kava is made from the roots and leaves of a kind of pepper plant. The method of preparation is interesting. Young boys and girls with sound teeth and excellent health are chosen for the honor of chewing the leaves. The leaves, well mashed, are spat out into a large bowl, and water and coconut milk are added and stirred vigorously. Then the woody parts are removed from the liquid. The result is a brownish or greenish drink, depending on whether roots or leaves have been used. The flavor of kava seems sweetish at first, then pungent and acid.

THE REINDEER HERDERS

The Lapp lives in the far north of Europe. Like the Eskimo, he has had to adapt his life to extreme winter cold, though Lapland is never as cold as where the Eskimo lives, nor is the land quite so bleak and barren. Also, like the Eskimo, the Lapp has developed a special way of living, and a very strange way it is.

The people of Lapland have made one big step toward civilization — from hunter to herdsman. This has meant a much easier and less dangerous way of getting food; it has also made for a safer and better food supply and a wider range of diet.

30

A Step Toward Civilization

Long ago, in prehistoric days, most human races began to domesticate either the horse or the cow, the sheep or the goat. But there are some lands where none of these animals can live. Lapland is one of them. The basis of the Lapp's life is one that is very strange to us; the reindeer.

The reindeer is closely related to the caribou of North America, and long ago the Lapp hunted the wild reindeer as the Eskimo hunts the caribou today. Then, at some unknown period in prehistory, he began to try to tame it. But the reindeer has never become truly tame, like the horse or cow; the process is still in the stage where the Lapp owner has to do as the reindeer wishes, and follow the herd; he cannot pen his reindeer and keep them in one place.

Twice a year the reindeer, like the caribou, takes it into his head to migrate. After the long, dark winter the grazing in the valleys is getting scarce and the biting flies are a torment. The female reindeer remembers where she was born and wants to return there; the male reindeer remembers the young and tasty birch shoots that grow only in the northern hills. Suddenly the herds gather together and head northward in one gigantic stampede.

The Lapp owner cannot head them off, but he has been expecting this migration. He has corralled a few of the older, part-broken animals, and now he hitches them, one each, to the canoe-shaped sleds. Women and children load their few possessions into the sleds, and leaving the grandparents to tend the small potato and barley patches already planted, they join the wild stampede. Already the men, on skis, with

31

Finnish Laplanders pause for a meal in the snow, between herding reindeer.

their dogs, are miles ahead, guarding the stragglers from wolves.

A few days later the reindeer reach their grazing grounds in the hills and spread out to feed on reindeer moss and young birch leaves. The family finds its usual summer campsite. Tent poles are brought out; tents are raised. The summer tent is called a *kata*. These were once of reindeer skins, but are now generally of cloth. The tent resembles an Indian wigwam and is family living room, bedroom and kitchen, throughout the summer. Around the campfire of twigs are arranged the few simple cookpots and the much-prized copper kettle. There is no chimney; the smoke from the fire goes out through the open top of the tent.

The main food is always reindeer meat. It was dried and frozen in the autumn of the previous year, when the herds had to be reduced in number, and is now thawed out, and chunks of it are tossed into the stewpot. Barley-meal dumplings and potatoes are added. There are big, wheel-like loaves of barley bread, which were frozen for easier carrying, and which are thawed when needed. There is also a thick pancake of batter, cooked on a hot stone, then turned to toast against the fire. This is called glowcake. Another special delicacy is the marrow from cracked reindeer bones.

Only a very few of the herd are tame enough to be milked, and the yield from one animal is little more than a cup a day. But the milk is as rich as cream and may be added to the coffee. Strong coffee, always ready in the pot, is heavily salted and is drunk many times a day. It is considered good manners to hold a lump of sugar between the teeth and suck the coffee through it, thus making the most of the costly sweetening.

Since the Lapp — like the Eskimo — is nomadic, he does not burden himself with tables and chairs in this summer camp. The floor covering is a thick layer of birch twigs, gathered freshly each week by the young daughter of the family; this keeps out the chill damp of the earth. Furs, and nowadays store blankets, are thrown down on it for sleeping, and are rolled up in the daytime. The Lapp family groups about the small, constantly burning fire to eat and gossip, as you would sit around a table. But they squat, or loll on one elbow.

The men always carry their own knives, as defense against bear or wolves or for cutting up a reindeer when slain. And as stew is the main dish, they also carry their own individual spoons.

There are no fixed mealtimes in the Lapp household. During midsummer the sun never sets — nor does it rise during midwinter, and days keep changing their length far more swiftly than they do farther south. It is not surprising that the Lapp is said to have little sense of time. Time doesn't really matter to him; the stewpot is always hot when he wants a

The Laplanders of Sweden toast glowcake beside the *kata* fire.

meal. The herdsman eats when he comes in from watching the reindeer; the women and children eat when they are hungry.

At the end of the summer, as the first snow falls, there is another stampede of the animals. They rush south this time, for their winter pasture is now free from the biting flies, and in the warmer valleys the reindeer moss is ready for grazing again. The herdsmen follow on skis. Skis, invented by the Lapps, are as necessary in reindeer herding as horses are on a cattle ranch.

The Lapp lives as far north as the Eskimo and has the same long, dark winters to contend with, but the Gulf Stream — which swings north of Europe — gives him a milder climate and a limited amount of scrub growth for fuel.

Since he has fuel to cook with, the Lapp has never had to eat raw meat, like the Eskimo, and since his people came north from southern Finland more recently in history than the Eskimos made their northern trek, he has not wholly adapted himself to a meat diet. He has fruits. One is a small cream-colored berry called dewberry, which tastes rather like our raspberry; and he has cranberries, smaller and sweeter than ours, which grow in the bogs and along the lakeshore.

What is most remarkable about the Lapp's life is that it is founded wholly on the reindeer; and the reindeer depend wholly on the reindeer moss. If grass had ever grown on these bleak, northern plains, other tribes would have driven in their cattle, fought the Lapp, and conquered him. But only the reindeer can exist on reindeer moss, and only the Lapp can follow the reindeer. All else — berries, barley, potatoes, hunting, trapping — would not have been enough to support him.

35

THE ARAB HERDSMEN

Until the opening of the Suez Canal in 1869, Arabia enjoyed a very profitable overland trade, carrying goods across the desert between the Mediterranean and the Indian Ocean. Even before this, the country was a link in the long caravan trade with China, through India and Persia and eastern Europe. Ruins, now engulfed in shifting sand, were once busy with commerce and lush with irrigated gardens. The memory of those past glories still colors the dreams of the town Arab as he sips his sweet brew in some roadside café.

36

In past centuries Arabia may have been even drier than it is today. Now a little barley is grown on the northern fringes of the country, fishing is carried on in the Red Sea and the Persian Gulf, and irrigation is beginning to finger its way into the wastelands. But the center of the country is waterless and without permanent dwellings. Nomad herdsmen graze their camels, horses and sheep over much of this area. Like the Lapp of the extreme north, the nomad Arab is entirely dependent on his livestock and the few date palms that grow at the scattered oases. Like the Lapp, also, he must go where his beasts can find forage, though the danger threatening him is not cold, but drought. The Arab has never completely emerged from nomad herding into farming and an agricultural life.

Desert Hospitality

There is a wide division between the village Arabs, no longer nomad wanderers, and the desert dwellers in tents. But though methods of cooking may vary greatly, both groups base their diets on the same basic foods — mutton and barley bread. And of course the universal coffee.

A desert tribe is really a clan, or family, or group living together in the black felt tents gathered about the oasis water hole with its tall date palms. Camels, sheep and horses spread out to graze where they can. The desert people live today much as they did in Biblical times; their diet and customs have altered little.

Since wood is scarce in the desert, the cook fire may be of palm branches, which give a hot, quick, but very smoky fire, or it may be the smoldering dried camel dung whose odor seeps everywhere. As soon as the family tents are set up, a small fire is started on the coffee hearth in the center of the main tent floor. This is for the men only. All other cooking is done in the women's section of the tent, shut off by a curtain.

The main dish is always mutton and rice, or chicken and rice, or camel meat and rice. Or just rice. For a real feast there would be a conical mountain of this rice, often four feet across and a foot high, drenched in greasy gravy. This pile is brought in on a copper platter by two tribal slaves, and will have taken all day to prepare. The hungry men, waiting, lounge back against the camel saddles on the floor while they sip very sweet mint-flavored tea, or toss off the thick, black coffee, served from a brass pot with a beaked snout.

As the tray is set down before the chief guest, who squats cross-legged on the floor, other eaters move in around it. A short prayer to Allah is murmured; then everyone starts to eat.

Around the main dish are arranged bowls of gravy, boiled chicken and various flavorings. All this has to be eaten with the hand, one hand only — always the right — though the other may be used to hold a chicken while the right pulls the carcass apart. Any hospitable host will kill a chicken for a guest, and often a sheep, or even a camel, whose boiled head, with gaping mouth to show the teeth, adorns the center of the tray. The eyeballs and pieces of hairy flesh from the ears are considered special delicacies.

"Eat like a camel and be the first to finish," is the Arab rule of good table manners. Every meal is an eating race; each

38

man crams himself feverishly and in silence, grasping the hot, sticky rice between thumb and palm, and thrusting it into his mouth. A ground-sheet has been spread over the eaters' laps, and whatever food falls into this cannot be recovered. At the end of the meal the right hand is coated with sticky rice

The nomad Arabs bake their unleavened bread on a stone or iron slab over a small open fire.

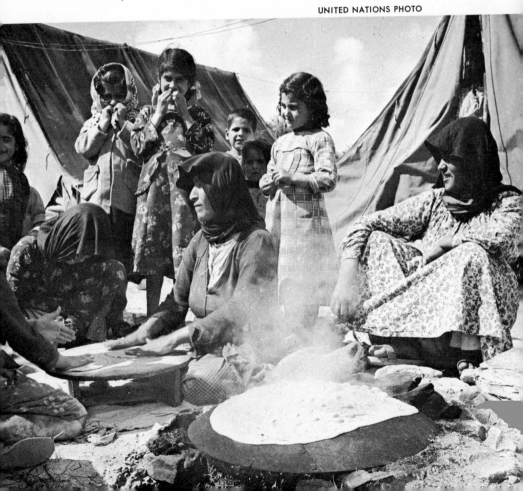

The Arab finds it more comfortable to sit on the ground and dine from a small, low table.

and grease. This must be licked off, but one must never lick the left hand.

Whatever food remains goes to the women's side of the tent; children and slaves are fed, and at last the waiting dogs, outside.

In all these countries where the women do the cooking but eat apart from the men, the cooks help themselves freely as they prepare the meal. The system is not as unfair to them as it appears to be. In lands where women still wear veils and never appear unveiled before strangers, they find it more comfortable to eat only with their own sex, where they can discard such inconvenience and formality.

The preparation and serving of coffee has its own rules of etiquette. The coffee beans must be freshly roasted over the fire in the presence of the guest, since no host would dream of offering stale coffee. It is then pounded with mortar and pestle, and the strong, thick coffee is freshly brewed. A servant or slave approaches the guest, with coffeepot in one hand, and a thimble-sized cup in the other. The small cupful must be tossed off, boiling hot, at one gulp. If the guest wishes more, he shakes the cup quickly as he returns it, but no more than three should be drunk at one time.

"Honor the guest, even though he be your enemy," is the strict Arab rule of hospitality. There is perhaps no community in the world that lives so habitually close to starvation as the desert nomad. But the best always belongs to the guest; the bread of yesterday's baking must never be offered him — even though in some households bread is so scarce that the women may only taste it three or four times in their lives. "This is the tent of bread" means "abundance."

The bread is unleavened, without yeast to raise the barley dough, and is in thin, pliable grayish sheets. The oven is

Coffee is a symbol of hospitality among the Arabs.

An Arab woman makes a fire in a baked-earth oven.

acorn shaped, of baked mud, with the top end open. The fire burns in the middle, and the dough is plastered on the inner walls of the oven. When scorched, it is pulled off in ragged sheets.

Town Arabs now use the primus stove; the older fuel was desert scrub or palm branches, which make a smoky fire. Charcoal braziers are also much used, and it is over such a brazier that the popular *kebab* is broiled. This consists of small pieces of lamb, threaded between bits of tomatoes and onions, on a metal skewer — like beads on a string. This is cooked, turning gently, over the charcoal fire. The charcoal was once kept glowing by a palm-leaf fan, but now an electric fan is often used instead.

42

The town dweller's oven is a truncated cone of clay in the open yard outside the house. The inside walls of this oven are of smooth plaster or porcelain. Here the fire of dry date-palm leaves is started, and when the oven is hot the ashes are raked out and large rounds of bread dough are slapped on the inside walls, to bake. These ovens are also used to cook a fish rather like our shad, which is split, cleaned and roasted, then served with a currylike paste. The season of this fish is in the spring, as with our shad, and throughout the riverside villages you can smell the delicious odor of its baking in almost every household oven.

Yoghurt is much used by the Arabs; it is called *robe*. In Lebanon it is called *lebben*. Another favorite dish is a milk pudding made with rice flour and flavored with rose water and cardamom seed, or one made with cracked wheat and flavored with *ghee*. Ghee is the oil from clarified butter.

Among the well-to-do town Arabs, the serving of a meal is a happy festivity. The celebration may be for a birth, or for a child's entry into his particular religious group, or for the cutting of a new tooth, and in some villages the celebration of his first year of life on earth. Adolescence and marriages are also occasions for feasts at which special delicacies are served, always accompanied by quantities of coffee.

Coffee originated in the Middle East and is drunk at any hour of the day. It is interesting how this custom of constant coffee drinking has spread up through Germany to Scandinavia and over into Iceland, where as many as thirty to forty cups a day may be consumed by a single person. In Arabia, coffee is served in a wide variety of cups, often with sweets and spices, and with a formality little less elaborate than that of the Japanese tea-drinking ceremony.

THE PEOPLE WHO STEPPED BACKWARD

There are many groups of people in the world who are slowly learning to conserve food, to herd their animals and fish, and to farm their lands efficiently. Also there are a few groups who were once fine farmers, with good herds of animals, who have returned to the primitive conditions of their remote ancestors. The reason for this return to primitive life will vary in different parts of the world, but as a rule the main reason is the land itself. The soil may have become impoverished; there may be a lack of water now, where once there was plenty; or the people themselves may have been so beaten down by conquerors that they no longer have the ability or the ambition to farm as they once did.

Farming seems to us a permanent way of life, and

we expect it to remain the same, with slow and steady improvement, century after century. But the farmer is not a warrior; he needs protection for his family, his flocks and his land, and if he is to farm for profit, he needs the roads and towns that make trade possible.

When the great Roman Empire was destroyed, the farming in its colonies was destroyed; the farms of England, of Spain, and particularly of France, were overrun and went back to their wild state. In time they recovered, but the Spanish destruction of the Inca Empire happened too recently for the Indians of the High Andes to have rebuilt their farms again. The Altiplano Indian inherited the remarkable food crops developed by his pre-Inca ancestors, along with the ruined cities of the Empire, but at present he seems incapable of regaining his past glories. He grows enough to live on, but no more.

Where the Corn Began

Around Lake Titicaca, in the towering Andes mountains of Peru, live several million Indians of the Quechua and Aymara tribes. They are quite unlike any Indians we know in North America. This altiplano, "high plateau," is a land of deep gorges and of gigantic, rugged peaks that tower to 20,000 feet; a bleak, windswept land, its higher slopes are treeless and waterless.

Before the Spanish Conquest, when the Incas ruled over all this land, the great staircase farms cherished every square foot of carefully fertilized and irrigated soil. Here were developed more varieties of food plants than in any other coun-

45

try of the same area in the world. Modern civilization owes much to these enlightened farmers who developed many varieties of maize; it is difficult to imagine modern American farming without our Indian corn.

The potato, which the Spaniards took to Europe, and Sir Walter Raleigh introduced to England, came from here. It was so important to Ireland that we still call it the Irish potato; and during the French Revolution this new vegetable fed France's starving peasants. It still appears on more dining tables in Europe and America than any other one vegetable.

Corn and potatoes are only two of the many vegetables, in everyday use, that came from this country. Sweet potatoes, certain kinds of gourds, lima beans, squash, cocoa, peanuts, tomatoes, cotton and tobacco, are all presumed to have been developed, over thousands of years, by the pre-Inca Indians, from wholly wild plants. It is said that the introduction of such South American species into Europe almost doubled the edible vegetables and useful plants.

The Inca Empire and its terraced farms are no more, and the miracle gardens that followed the contours of the steep mountain sides are in ruins — like the great temples and fortresses. The Indian, the direct descendant of the specialists who gave us the maize and potato, is incredibly enduring, but today he is poverty-stricken and without initiative.

There are a few traces of the past glories. Maize is still grown in many varieties unknown to the north. And where else would you find a corncob with grains an inch across, which can be eaten one at a time, like chestnuts? Potatoes are also still a most important food to these people, and are strangely preserved by drying. They are laid out in the cold mountain air to freeze and thaw, and old men, women and

In the High Andes, the women and old men pound out the frozen potatoes with their feet.

A farmer's wife in Peru grinds corn by hand.

children trample them underfoot to press out all the juice. The result, called *chuno,* is carried in small woolen bags as a staple meal for the herdsmen. They sprinkle chuno on their thin breakfast gruel, and mix it with their dinner of boiled-down vegetables.

The Indian's main food is still maize. Wheat has been introduced from Europe and grows in the lowlands. There is *quinua* also, a ricelike grain. And, growing in the high mountains, is an herb like our pigweed or lamb's-quarters. Meat is very scarce, and the lakes and streams produce few fish.

Life in the lowlands is less rigorous, and the farms there are more rewarding. Oxen pull a clumsy, primitive plow made of a bough that is nowadays tipped with iron. Tough little donkeys serve as pack beasts, to carry the heavy loads. But at greater heights the donkey and ox cannot live, so men are forced to cultivate the land with crude digging sticks, and act as their own beasts of burden. They can also pack light loads on the small, ill-tempered and only half-tamed llama. Here also herds of vicuñas and alpacas, smaller relatives of the llama, are raised for their fine wool and a meager supply of meat, and the alpaca yields a little milk. All meat is dried in the dry mountain air, chopped fine, and sprinkled into the stew, to make it go farther. This stew is highly seasoned with *aji*, a kind of hot chili pepper, or with spicy berries.

In the lowland valleys, wood for the cook fire is easily obtained. But in the mountains dried grass, twisted into tight ropes, or llama dung is used. The odor of this seeps into all food, and even into the clothing.

Kitchen and eating utensils are limited to a pottery pot or two, or an occasional modern iron cookpot, tin plates and gourd spoons. Cooking is still done by dropping very hot stones into the pot, to bring the stew to a boil. The houses, of fieldstone or adobe brick, stone floored, are very poor and without furniture.

There are only two meals a day. One remarkable custom is that the Indian does not like to be seen eating, and when forced to eat in public, will sit facing the wall, hunched well over his eating bowl.

Every Indian chews *coca* — not cocoa, but a drug with effects somewhat like opium. This allays hunger, thirst, and the fatigue of carrying heavy loads up and down steep trails. But today the Altiplano Indians are no longer noted farmers; they are herdsmen, mountaineers and beasts of burden.

49

THE PUEBLO PEOPLE

The American Indians of our Southwest were originally hunters and foragers. Some kept flocks of wild turkeys, but these were sacred birds; it was their plumage that was important to the tribe, not their flesh. Like most foragers living within reach of more fruits in season than they could eat, the early Indians developed many clever ways of conserving: they sun-dried the pulp; they parched the seed; they boiled down the juices. This was an important advance from haphazard gathering. So far as we know, no desert Indians of the Southwest were able to take the next step toward an agricultural civilization. They did not sow the wild seed of any plant so as to improve its strain by selection of the best. It is probable that lack of water and constant tribal wars made such experiments nearly impossible.

Later, well before the white man came, they had inherited maize, pumpkins and beans from Central America. Such agricultural improvements must have come north slowly, over hundreds of years, through trade and barter. The tribes continued to forage and hunt, and it was not until the Spanish brought goats, and, more important, sheep, to the pueblo country that these people became true herdsmen. Foragers and hunters, being nomad people, must content themselves with temporary houses; they cannot carry around such heavy implements as stone grills, or make permanent fireplaces.

With agriculture — and even the cliff dwellers raised corn — came improvements in cooking arrangements. And with better equipment, better food followed. Pottery became an advance over the earlier clay-lined basket into which hot stones must be dropped to cook the stew. Better pottery could be set directly on the fire. And with better ovens came better bread, though as yet unleavened.

The Corn Comes North

Of the American Indians who live in our desert Southwest, those known as the Pueblos seem to be the furthest advanced in agriculture. *Pueblo,* meaning "town," was the name given them by the conquering Spanish, because of their large mud-walled and many-storied settlements.

As with nearly all American Indians, the diet is based on maize. This was named Indian corn by our ancestors, since the Indian first taught the New England settlers to grow and prepare it. The ancient cultivation of it is so important to the Pueblo people that most of their religion consists of propitiation of the corn gods, and of the rain gods whose blessing is so necessary for a good harvest.

The outdoor adobe ovens, resembling large beehives, are landmarks around the Indian pueblos of New Mexico.

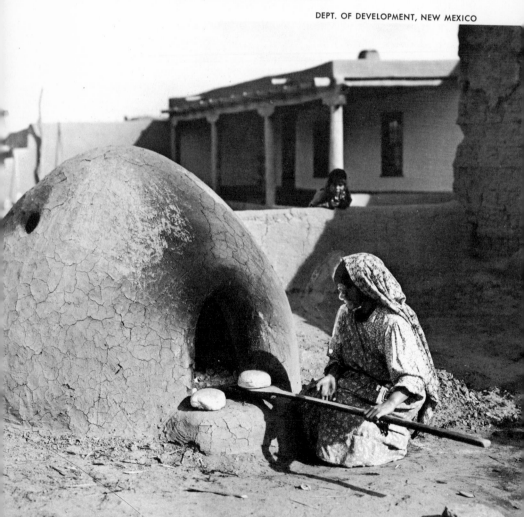

Corn is a plant that cannot compete with weeds, and was cultivated with much labor, using a wooden digging stick. Indian villages practiced irrigation from very early days; they made channels to bring the water to their small plots. They held elaborate ceremonies and dances in which they begged

An Indian woman grinds corn as her ancestors did a thousand years ago.

the gods for favorable growing weather and for good crops. Lima beans, pumpkin and squash were planted among the corn. Many of the tribes were hunters as well as farmers, so there was venison, buffalo and other game with which to augment the diet. When the Spanish brought sheep, the herds increased, and as wild game became scarce the mutton was a valuable addition to the cookpot.

In the desert the main fuels are mesquite and algaroba, two similar shrubs which burn easily and well. Cactus is used, too, especially one named "Spanish dagger," and pine and other woods are available in the mountains. In the pueblo houses much of the cooking can be done indoors; the fireplace in the corner of the room, raised slightly from the floor, has a hood which carries the smoke to a chimney. In another corner of the room stand the slab-lined meal bins, with their *metates*, tablelike stones with concave upper surfaces, for grinding the corn. The corn must first be sun-dried on the flat housetops, then treated with lye to remove the chaff. Finally it is ground by hand between the cylindrical roller and the stone metate slab.

It is from this coarse flour or cornmeal that the popular *tortilla* is made. Tortillas are flat corn cakes and are baked on a stone slab, as they have been for centuries, though sometimes today a metal sheet is used over an open fire. There are also delicious crisp cakes called *piki,* paper-thin sheets of maize bread, which keep for days. These can be rolled around a piece of meat, goat's-milk cheese or piñon nuts. Larger tortillas — from twelve to sixteen inches across —are not patted out by hand, as in Mexico, but are thrown from arm to arm, to flatten the dough before cooking.

Nowadays wheat flour is also used, baked into loaves in the outdoor ovens. There are usually two of these beehive-shaped ovens outside the house. The venthole lets the smoke out of the top; the small open doorway at the bottom can be closed with a board. The fire inside is allowed to burn until the oven walls are very hot, then the ashes are raked out, and the bottom of the oven swabbed with a wet cloth on a long pole, so that no ash will adhere to the dough. The bread is not baked in pans, but the shaped mounds are slashed halfway through with a knife, so that the finished loaf looks as though it had five fingers. It is slid into the oven on smooth, flat boards, and a board covered with a wet cloth covers the entrance hole again. Another wet cloth stops the venthole at the top.

The bread takes about a half hour to bake, and comes out beautifully crusty and brown. The slashed-off pieces break away easily so that the loaves need not be sliced.

Tamales, enchiladas, and other combinations of cornmeal and meat, vary considerably from tribe to tribe and village to village. Pumpkin, squash and beans are stewed with meat or gravy, and eaten with the tortilla, which serves as both fork and spoon.

In the early days, as with all hunting peoples, the women not only did all the cooking, but were also the gardeners. Meals were served first to the men; then the women squatted around the stew to eat with the children. Today the whole family may eat together, as we do, and there is less and less difference between their eating and ours. Such families as can afford it, purchase coffee, which they drink in great quantities, and canned fruit and candies from the grocery. Old tribal customs and foods are rapidly becoming things of the past.

HEIRS OF THE AZTECS

The Spanish conquest of Peru destroyed the vast
and elaborate civilization of the Incas and left nothing in its place. The destruction of the Aztec Empire
in Mexico was as complete, but its results were not
so far reaching. In the milder climate and more fertile
land, a simpler, less organized agriculture continued
without a break. And the Spanish conquerors stayed
on, to mingle with the Indian population. They introduced European livestock, and where conditions
permitted, more modern methods of farming.

The area made no special contributions to agriculture, such as had come from ancient Peru, but its
future prospects are brighter. There are large tracts
where progressive farming may be used, and only
the apathy of the people and absentee landlordism
stand in the way of advancement.

The Meals of Mexico and Central America

Mexico, and Central America, from which stem so much of our North American Indian agriculture and pottery, is also the ancestor of Indian cooking in the Southwest. Pure Indians are less than a third of Mexico's population, and pure whites are still rarer, so the vast majority is of mixed blood. But the Mexican and Central Americans still prefer the food and customs that existed before the Spanish Conquest in the sixteenth century.

This may be because the soil was generally fertile; there were then, as there are today, many fruits and vegetables to choose from, and a wide variety of dishes to make from them. Maize is of course the mainstay; with squash, tomatoes, beans, onions, and many tropical fruits, to add flavor. Cheese made from goat's milk is also important in the diet.

The main fuel is charcoal. Wood is not scarce, but the almost smokeless charcoal is more suitable for the peasants' primitive cooking. In the larger households, wood-burning stoves are preferred; these are long, boxlike affairs of clay and tile, open at one end to receive the fuel, and topped by a single row of iron lids that resemble those on old-fashioned New England cookstoves. But even in these more prosperous households, a charcoal brazier is used to augment the cookstove.

The "bread" of Mexico, and of all Central American countries, is the tortilla. This is made from corn, prepared much as the Southwest Indians prepare it. The woman kneels before a metate, places a handful of grain on it, and with a stone rolling pin, pounds and rolls the grain into a coarse meal.

Tortillas are an important part of the diet in Central America. Here an Indian of Guatemala grinds corn on a *metate*.

The meal is then mixed with a little water and salt. Small brown hands take a lump from the pottery container, shape it into a ball, and slap and pat it into a thin pancake — you can hear this constant *slap, slap,* all day long in any Mexican village. The flat tortilla is cooked on a wide pottery disk, over a low fire. These delicious pancakes may be eaten hot, plain, wrapped about a cheese or meat filling, or used to mop up

Guatemala. An Indian family patting tortillas into shape for baking.

the last bits of food on a plate. Or, cold, they are carried in a little woven bag, when the laborer goes to work in the field.

The tortilla of maize is the basis of life, but it takes so long to turn the corn from cob into cornmeal that many estate owners have now installed mechanical mills. But, for a long time, the slapping of tortillas will continue to be a pulsebeat of life in Central America.

Frijoles, beans of various kinds, are as old a food as maize and furnish a cheap protein that is lacking in the pure corn-meal diet. They are boiled in earthenware pots, and flavored with herbs, a meat sauce, or tomatoes, peppers and onions.

Added to the diet of tortillas and beans are whatever fruits the land produces; these may be bananas of many kinds, avocados, papaws and oranges. For the well-to-do there are pork, chicken, eggs and goat's meat; there is seldom sufficient grazing to support cows.

The most popular drink is cocoa. The powdered cocoa is mixed with sugar and cinnamon and shaped into little cooky-like cakes, which are then dried in the sun. To make the drink, hot milk is poured into a bright-colored wooden mug, a cake is dropped into this, and a small wooden notched stick is whirled between the palms of the hands, to beat it into a frothy beverage. Coffee is also a favorite drink.

There are other *refrescos,* "refreshing drinks," of fruit juices sweetened with honey and brown sugar; and there are hot herb drinks such as camomile tea, and a tea made from the dried leaves of oregano, or of sage.

Mexico and Central American countries have an unusual classification of foods into *hot* and *cold.* This, surprisingly, has nothing to do with the temperature of the food itself. The hot foods are so called because they are believed to stimulate

60

heat in the body; the cold foods are considered more difficult to digest, and hence they are cooling. The hot foods are beef, honey and coffee, and are thought to be good for chills; cold foods, recommended for fevers, are turkey, rice, boiled eggs, limes and pork. Hot and cold foods may cause an illness, or cure one, through their effect on the heat or cold of the body.

El Salvador. A type of stove in common use.

AFRICANS AT HOME

It was a big step forward in civilization when families ceased following their herds and became settled farmers. Naturally this did not happen all at the same time and all over the world, in fact it is still going on in many places, as you have seen. It took place here and there and gradually, and it is possible that women were the first to dig in the soil with crude digging sticks, and to hopefully plant the seeds that they would harvest later in the year.

Africa is an enormous continent. Even today, its various tribes — widely separated in their culture — represent every step in the progress from foraging to food growing; from the South African Bushman, through the nomad cattle-raising Fulah and the sheep-raising Arab of the north, to the settled farmers throughout the country. The truly successful farmer raises food not only for his own family, on a subsistence farm, but has a crop of one kind of another which he can trade with his neighbors, or can carry to some nearby market to swap for other foods, or for salt, cloth, pottery and tools.

The sample of Africa which we have taken is Nigeria, on the west coast. This country measures nearly 1,000 miles from west to east, and some 800 miles from north to south. It ranges from the steaming equatorial forests of the south to the arid north where little but camel-thorn — a spiny shrub — will grow. So even here in this corner of Africa the people raise many different kinds of foodstuffs; have many distinct cooking and eating customs. We describe those who inhabit the widest area.

The Step to Agriculture

Nigeria, once part of the British Colonial Empire, and now divided into three sections, each with its own government, is still one of the largest countries in the British Commonwealth. Among the tribes that live along the Atlantic coast, fish and root crops are the main diet. Inland, in what is called bush country — because it bears only small, stunted trees — the people farm and raise *millet*.

Millet resembles our maize, or Indian corn, when it is growing, but the seeds form into loose tufts rather than cobs. And all over this part of Africa the little villages resound with what sounds like drumming as the women beat out this millet with big, heavy pestles in hollowed logs. This pounding is to

The Hausa women of Nigeria pound grain in a big wooden mortar. There is a constant sound of these drumbeats in all African villages.

loosen the chaff, sticks and waste, from the seed. It is then winnowed in the breeze, to blow this away. The remaining grain is ground to a coarse meal on a stone trough, with a stone rolling pin. Millet is the main food of many millions of people, not only in West Africa but in the south and east.

It can be eaten in several ways. The simplest is the one used by travelers on the road. They sprinkle a little of the raw meal into their calabash water bottles and drink it as a thin gruel. It may be mixed with water, rolled into balls about the size of small plums and dropped into a hot stew to cook. These little dumplings, spiced with one of the many native flavorings, are then picked out with the fingers of one hand only, and popped into the mouth. Or the balls may be covered with gravy made from meat, or just dusted over with more flour, and eaten plain. Sometimes the coarse flour is made into a porridge, and if the cook lives near the coast, flavored with coconut oil; or with palm oil, which comes from trees nearer inland; or with peanut oil in the north. Fats and oils are important additions to the diet. Such porridge is eaten with a small gourd, or a wooden spoon.

Since Nigeria is a hot country, the people do not need much meat, nor is there much available. In the wilder parts people shoot or trap game and bring it home to the cook. A small boy, lucky enough to bag a bird or other small game, will sometimes cook and eat it by himself in the bush. When a hunter kills something big, like a hippopotamus, there is more than enough for everyone, and no means of preserving the meat before it spoils. Then men, women and children seem to scent the prize from afar, and gather from all the surrounding countryside. But such luck is rare, and most people are nearly vegetarian — not from choice but from necessity.

The Mohammedans of the northern and central parts of Nigeria don't keep pigs or eat pork. Though there are many kinds of cattle, very little beef is eaten. The tall, humped Fulah cattle of the north furnish milk, but this is never drunk raw. In fact they will tell you that fresh milk is poisonous. They collect the milk into large calabashes or wooden bowls, and drop into it a "magic" stone, which is often a stone ax-head. The stone is taken from already soured milk, and carries the culture over to the fresh milk, making it sour. The milk may then be kept for some time, and is safe from air-borne germs. No one knows how long this has been going on, or who invented the system. But the stone axhead must date back hundreds and perhaps thousands of years.

Goat meat is popular, and many families keep a few goats. Like other meat, it is mostly used for flavoring millet meal, to make it stretch further. When cooked by itself, it is often broiled on skewers over an open wood fire, and the fat and juices are carefully caught for future cooking. Camels, horses and donkeys are ridden in one part of the country or another, but are not eaten.

A big clay pot, partly buried in the ground, serves for an outdoor oven. A smaller pot, balanced on stones, is used for ordinary cooking over a small open fire. Cooking is done by women and outdoors if the weather permits. Where a man may have several wives — as among the Mohammedans — it is an honor to cook, and each wife will take her turn.

You might think that this diet would be rather monotonous, as so much of it is based on millet meal or an almost flavorless root called *cassava*. But the cook uses different herbs, many unknown in other countries. In Northern Nigeria, there is one very favorite spice which comes from the sugary pod of a tree

In Africa the men do not eat with the women.

like a locust tree. Sugarcane is often grown, and there is also a millet whose stem holds sweet juices. Wild honey is greatly prized, and some tribes put hollow logs in trees to attract the bees. As is always true where people live largely on vegetables, salt is most important and has always been a valuable article of trade. In the old days rock salt was brought in on camel back from the Sahara Desert, to be sold in the markets in red or brown crystal blocks. Even today, most people prefer this to the cheaper white salt of commerce; they say it has more flavor.

In Ghana, the West African housewife prepares the meal over a small outdoor fire.

Usually the Nigerian eats only two meals a day; breakfast shortly after dawn, and dinner after the sun drops near the horizon, when the day's work is over and it is cool enough to enjoy the food. The men may eat separately, when they return from farming or hunting, and the women take snacks

68

during the day, but in some tribes the men and women eat together.

Northern Nigerians are great travelers. They love to pack up suddenly and go on a journey. They call this "drinking the breeze." The men of some tribes are wandering traders, carrying their goods on their heads. Because of this, many little roadside markets spring up, with small huts or stalls of sun-baked mud and straw thatching, where different kinds of sugar candy, peanuts, and other small snacks, as well as substantial food, may be bought cheaply.

A whole family may decide to go on a long journey, each child and adult carrying a heavy load, the smallest toddler carrying something light, like an empty calabash. They travel slowly, and mostly during the cool of the night, but go tremendous distances. Some will cross the whole of Africa, taking years over the journey, and perhaps stopping on the way to plant and reap a harvest or two.

Except among the rich and modern, living conditions are very simple. There are no tables and chairs; everyone squats on the ground or on mats when eating. A big clay pot for an oven, a smaller clay pot for general cooking, and nowadays a small tin kettle for boiling water, are all the kitchen equipment required. Gourd bowls of different shapes and sizes serve for dishes, plates and spoons, and are home grown in the garden and whittled into shape by the men. Threshing the grain with the mortar and pestle, winnowing the seed from the chaff on a tray, and finally grinding the corn into meal or coarse flour, take up much of a woman's day. The actual cooking and eating is a very simple matter for everyone, both cook and diners.

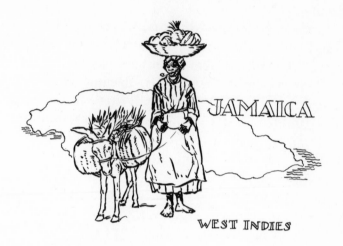

AFRICANS FAR FROM HOME

The beautiful islands of the West Indies are too numerous to be listed here. The most tropical are Jamaica, Hispaniola, Puerto Rico, the Leeward and Windward islands and Trinidad. These lie in the Caribbean Sea, southeast of the United States, east of Mexico and Central America.

Most of the Carib and Arawak Indians, who lived here before Columbus and the Spanish landed on the islands, vanished long ago. The various European races who conquered and colonized them, brought with them their own foods and ways of cooking. They also brought many kinds of fruits and vegetables not native to the island or other islands. The result is that food customs and cooking vary widely from is-

70

land to island, and may remind you of the dishes of Spain, Holland, Scotland, England, France, Denmark, and even India and China.

Each island is a separate "melting pot," a miniature of a multiracial city such as New York. Yet in each one the population is largely African in origin; and the foods of the farmers, the peasants, are more like those in West Africa than in any other single country. Even the language is colored by the African dialects brought in by the slaves two hundred years ago, and is often quite incomprehensible to the visitor. Both languages and foods are a triumph of strong racial characteristics over completely alien environments.

Relaxed Meals in the West Indies

Like the people themselves, the foodstuffs and cooking customs of the West Indies are imported from many parts of the world. In the early days, when the white men settled there, sugar was such a profitable crop that other food growing was neglected. The daily rations which the plantation owner was bound by law to give his slaves were brought from the coasts of North America — mainly dried or salt fish. This was exchanged with New England for sugar and rum. Fishing fleets out of Nova Scotia and New England had brought in cod for drying for many generations and fish-drying had become an industry. Each slave was also given a patch of ground on which to grow his own crops, and was allowed one day a week to work it. He was as much a stranger to the West Indies as his European master, and was seldom a good farmer. To prepare his ground, he hacked down bushes and trees and

In the Caribbean Islands, the diet is largely vegetarian. Yams are especially well liked.

The women walk to market to exchange their vegetables for eggs and perhaps a fowl. The men ride!

burned them. This gave a good first crop, but allowed the topsoil to wash away, and this wasteful custom still continues in most of the islands.

The usual crops grown in the small home gardens are beans, yams, sweet potatoes, and the starchy root called cassava that we heard of in Nigeria, which has to be grated and the pulp carefully washed to rid it of its poisonous juices. Corn and sugarcane are also grown in small patches, and a kind of rice that will grow in dry soil. Bananas flourish almost everywhere and there are many varieties, small and large, yellow and red, and one which cannot be eaten raw but must

AMADOR PACKER

A discarded gasoline tin makes a good cooking vessel, or even a stove, in Jamaica.

be cooked. Papaw trees, with their oblong, yellow, applelike fruit, spring up from seed even in the towns. There are many kinds of oranges, grapefruit, lemons and limes. Jack fruit, the seeds of which are roasted and eaten, custard apples and sweetsop have soft, creamy pulps which may be spooned out and eaten, but soursop is a pear-shaped fruit which has flesh like cotton batting, from which the juice must be pressed for flavoring. The naseberry, which usually grows wild in fencerows, has flesh which looks and tastes rather like roasted apples. Northern apples, pears and similar American fruits do not thrive in the tropics.

Coconut palms, tall and feathery, grow best along the shore, but there are large plantations of them farther inland. There are many kinds. Coir, a fiber made from the outer husks of coconuts, is used for matting. The juice of the unripe coconut is a delightful drink, but the ripe nut is still more valuable. Grated nut is eaten with curries, or cooked in other dishes. Cream is made by pressing the grated nut, or cooking oil may be extracted in a similar way.

Breadfruit was brought to Jamaica by Captain Bligh, famous for the mutiny on his ship *Bounty*. It was introduced from the South Sea Islands, as food for slaves. The slaves disliked it. It is now highly prized throughout the Caribbean, and is eaten, like potatoes, as a vegetable, though it grows on big trees. The *akee* is said to come from Africa. The trees grow to a great height and bear a yellow fruit which turns scarlet when ripe. Inside the red husks are black seeds in yellow flesh, and the flesh, when boiled, tastes and looks somewhat like scrambled eggs. Salt-fish with akee is a very popular dish nowadays, though slaves once went on strike rather than eat it.

On the larger islands there are extensive cattle estates in the cool uplands. There are no sheep; but goats may be seen on every roadside. Many families keep a pig which eventually becomes food and thus atones for the damage it has done in rooting up the family vegetables. Some have skinny chickens, which are expected to forage for themselves, and are seldom fed. There is no lack of different kinds of meat, but prices are high, so the poorer people are almost vegetarian. Near the coast, fish makes up for this lack.

Sugarcane is still the main crop and the main export. Everyone chews cane during the season, and the markets and roadsides are littered with its spat-out pulp. Colored drinks made of sugar and local flavorings, poured over shaved ice, are sold from barrows and stalls wherever laborers are employed.

Except during the heavy rains, all cooking is done outdoors, sometimes in a five-gallon oilcan, or in a three-legged cast-iron caldron. In Jamaica, this pot is called a *do-mek-a-see,* "don't let me see," perhaps because it has a lid. Outdoors a small fire is kindled between supporting rocks, but indoors a charcoal brazier, called a coalpot, is preferred; it gives off no smoke, and affords a steadier heat.

Favorite dishes vary greatly from island to island and according to the racial background of the cook. In Jamaica, a universal dish is "hopping John," rice cooked with black peas and bacon and seasoned with red pepper. *Duckanoo,* which is cornmeal and green bananas, flavored with currants, tied up in a banana leaf and dropped into boiling water, is also much liked. *Bammee* is made with grated cassava meal formed into a flat cake and soaked in milk before frying. Green bananas are crushed with coconut oil and cooked; this makes a food, even for babies. The Chinese and East Indians have brought many recipes from their homelands, but the simplest Jamaican dish of all is a cold boiled yam left from the previous day, eaten by a laborer on his way to work or by a child going to school.

The main meal of the day, which is in the evening, may be eaten at table with spoon and knife, or seated on the ground and eaten with a big iron spoon from a tin plate or a bowl, as we eat our breakfast cereal. There are no fixed hours for eating. These are the easygoing tropics.

THE PEASANTS OF INDIA

It is said of India, as of China and Africa, that "Anything reported may be true. Nothing reported can be universally true." This is because all three countries are so vast and because each contains the greatest possible contrasts between wealth and poverty, between elaborate luxury and complete simplicity.

Like many countries in the East, India is discarding its old customs. The well-to-do families send their children to France or England to school, or hire teachers from Europe, and at home they live much as we do. Men and women eat together; they dine from tables, with silver and linen, and their food varies little from European food.

This is not true of the peasants. The peasant of India has never had an easy life. The country is increasingly overpopulated, debt ridden, short of land for farming, and has an ever-mounting taxation. It is possible that modern government irrigation may alter the peasant's lot somewhat, but today he still lives very much from hand to mouth, close to starvation.

Chupatties, Curry and Coconuts

Among India's swarming millions, cooking and eating customs have not altered in hundreds of years. Variation comes only from section to section of the country, and the curries of the north are not the curries of the south, east or west. There is also a religious difference in diets; Hindus do not eat beef, since the cow is sacred; Mohammedans are forbidden to eat pork. There are many kinds of fruits and vegetables. Nothing is served in its natural form; all fruits or vegetables are chopped or ground very fine and mixed with spices, sugar, honey, or other fruits and vegetables.

The "bread" of India is the *chupatti*. When a housewife makes chupatties, which she cooks fresh each day, she visits the market place and spends a few pennies for a handful or two of wheat. She carries this, wrapped in a corner of her *sari*, her dress, to the miller, who is also in the native market place. He grinds the wheat in a little handmill, retaining part of the coarse flour in payment.

The chupatti is made by kneading this whole-wheat flour with a little water and butter. This is swiftly rolled into small balls of dough, about six inches thick, which are held over the charcoal stove, where they swell like small balloons. Turned

78

over, they swell again, which finishes the cooking. They are then flattened, with a hard slap on a board, and anointed with more butter. They are served in a high pile, like pancakes, from which the eater helps himself, using the chupatti like a scoop or spoon for his other foods.

Cooking is almost always the task of the women. Meals are served to the men first. No tables are used; the men sit in a line on the floor of the porch, or around the outdoor fire.

A kitchen in India, with the main meal of the day in preparation.

The dish may be a big brass plate, a banana leaf or a bowl, and all eating is done neatly, with the fingers.

All food is placed before the diner at the same time; nothing is very hot or very cold. On the big brass plate may be a small mound of *neem-tree* leaves, which look and taste a little like spinach, a large mound of rice, some puffed pastry shells — fried pastries called *puries* — a small fish cooked with head and tail intact, some fried cauliflower, and a curry of spicy vegetables and meats. Grouped around this main dish is a circle of small brass bowls containing curried shrimps, cottage cheese mixed with potato, and some runny rice called *payas* mixed with nuts and pieces of fruit.

Curry is called "the salt of the East," and was probably originally devised to hide the flavor of meat, which does not keep well in hot countries. These curries vary greatly from district to district; some are very hot and peppery, some are a little sweet. Spices are never used singly, and there may be a combination of as many as sixteen different flavorings, all skillfully blended, in recipes that have come down in the family from generation to generation.

India is rich in fruits; mangos, bananas, oranges, lemons, jack fruit, peaches, and many kinds of nuts. The coconut is specially prized as an accompaniment to curry, for its oil, and as a basis for many sweetmeats.

You can see that in such a torrid country as India people like their foods strongly flavored. This is partly because spices are easily obtained in such countries, but also because a diet based almost wholly on root crops and grains is flat and flavorless. People in cold climates, who live largely on meat, feel no need for such strong flavorings, and in a cold climate the appetite does not need much stimulation.

An old kerosene tin makes an excellent charcoal stove in this Indian household.

CHINA

THE PEOPLE OF THE CHOPSTICK COUNTRIES

In the countries you have heard about so far, all the eating has been done with the fingers, or with knife and spoon. Now we come to a very odd eating tool, chopsticks. Nobody knows how ancient is the custom of eating with chopsticks, but this means of conveying food to the mouth must be very old indeed, since the Japanese brought chopsticks with them when, hundreds of years ago, they crossed over from the mainland of China.

JAPAN

Perhaps chopsticks originated because hard metal to fashion individual knives, such as nomad hunters and herdsmen always carry, was not easily obtained. Some tool was needed to pick up the food, yet keep the fingers clean.

Chopsticks are long, slender sticks of wood, and come in pairs. A set of bamboo sticks may be served fresh with each meal, or the eater may carry his own set. Between meals he thrusts this into a small case at his belt. The use of the sticks requires practice and skill, but then so does the use of knife and fork. Chopsticks are held in one hand. Two fingers grasp the upper stick against the thumb; the other two move the lower stick, much as the lower jaw moves against the upper in chewing. One is stationary, the other mobile. The bowl of rice or other food is held in the other hand, close to the mouth. With chopsticks, the diner can transfer food swiftly from bowl to mouth, and all food is specially prepared to fit this method of eating.

Eating by Numbers in Japan

Japan is a series of small and densely populated islands. For centuries, and by its own wish, it was cut off from contact with the rest of the world. No foreign wars, no epidemics, kept down the population growth. The result was too little land and too many farmers.

One effect of this was to produce one of the most intensive and efficient systems of cultivation the world has ever known. A second effect was to evolve an elaborate but economical

At a wedding reception the newlyweds partake of many exotic foods from tiny individual tables.

preparation of foods. The third was to create a gracious formality of manners, designed to smooth away the annoyance of living in very close communities. Household goods are few, but of delicate beauty and perfection. And as though to take the place of other occupations and amusements for which there is little scope, the eating of meals is exceedingly formal and ceremonious. The process of eating in Japan is perhaps the most specialized dining ritual in the world.

Though the people of Japan originally came from China,

their foods and ways of cooking are quite different. Almost the only thing the two countries have in common is the use of chopsticks, and the fact that dishes in both countries must be prepared for eating with these tools.

In Japan the appearance of the food is of great importance. Everything is laid down by rules. The size and shape of the individual tray on which it is served; the color arrangement of the food and dishes on that tray — even the number of them — all have a special meaning. Perhaps this is because the Japanese have learned to make much of little and to eat many things that would seem unsatisfying and sometimes even unpleasant. So the cook pays even more attention to what food looks like than to what it tastes like.

Many foods are pickled in brine, only slightly cooked, or even served raw. Cooking is done over a charcoal brazier; the housewife uses a little fan to keep the fire glowing hot. Some dishes are even prepared at table, before the guest, like our chafing-dish cookery, and only the women are cooks.

Family and guests remove their shoes when they enter the house, and kneel on large, square cushions before individual little tables. In early Japan, metal was scarce and difficult to mine, so craftsmen created a special kind of lacquered wood for bowls and trays. These are simple and beautiful in shape, usually of black or a rich, soft red, and decorated in gold or silver designs. They can withstand great heat.

Three or five dishes, always an odd — not an even — number, are brought in on the guest's tray. Rice is the main dish, with soup and a boiled vegetable or boiled fish or meat. If the tray holds five dishes, the other two will be a vegetable pickled in vinegar or boiled greens with soy sauce. If the meal is a real feast, there will be still another two dishes, making

A small boy eats with chopsticks from his rice bowl. His home is on a *junk* in Hong Kong Harbor.

seven in all. These two will be sliced raw fish and pickles. Each serving has its special color arrangement and its own place on the tray, as prescribed by etiquette.

The guest makes a slight bow and remarks, "I start eating." He then removes the lid of the rice bowl, holding the bowl in his one hand, the lid in the other. The soup bowl is uncovered in the same way, but reversing the hands. Chopsticks are then picked up, with the same studied gesture, and soup and rice are scooped up alternately.

It is not polite to eat food other than rice without eating rice also, and care must be taken in holding the bowl so that any food that slips off the chopsticks falls back into the dish. Nor is it considered good manners to eat less than two bowls of rice at a meal . . . if you wish a third, you must also eat a fourth bowl.

A fish, served whole, faces to the left, and must be eaten so as to leave the bones in the same position.

The final dish is pickles; Japanese do not care for sweet things. Pickles come after all other food is consumed, and it is impolite to eat anything after that.

When the meal is over, the tips of the chopsticks are dipped in hot water, wiped with a small piece of paper, and replaced on the tray in the same position in which they were brought in. The guest then gives a little bow, saying "Goshiso sama." "It was quite a treat."

The only drinks served with a meal are tea and *sake*. Sake is a wine made of fermented rice, and served warm from little individual bottles.

The tea ceremony of Japan does not accompany the usual meal, but is a ritual of hospitality which is very formal and ceremonious. It is planned for eyes, nose and palate, and both host and guests enjoy it to the full. A special group of beautiful utensils is used; the tea is made fresh from water boiling over a small charcoal brazier, incense perfumes the air, and the hostess kneels on a mat to welcome her guests. The guest, who is also kneeling, receives the tea as it is poured into a small handleless cup. Every movement of all parties is as ritually performed as a dance, and each gesture must be beautifully exact.

Some sweetmeats are eaten and these may be almond cakes or candied fruit. Before sipping from the cup, the guest carries it to his forehead, in token of respect. She then persuades her hostess to drink, by moving the hostess' cup nearer to her hand. The tea must be consumed in three and a half long sips; the last sip with a low sound of appreciation. Then another cup is poured.

Rice, eaten with chopsticks, is good at any hour of the day and on any Chinese street.

This all sounds most elaborate, and it is; far more than is outlined here. The tea ceremony is very old; it is supposed to give rise to beautiful thoughts on the part of both hostess and guest. The ritual, usually for five persons, takes place in a special room of the house — a room designed just for the tea ceremony, and called *cha-na-yu* by the Japanese. It has come down today, almost unaltered, since the fifteenth century.

Nowadays the Japanese are beginning to use Western-style chairs and tables, and to install modern kitchens in which to cook their meals. It is a pity to see the graceful old customs dying out.

Black Eggs and Bird's-nest Soup in China

China is so vast a country that its range of climate and soil and hence foodstuffs is very wide. The people vary widely also, but many of the basic foods are the same. In the past it was not racial differences, but those of climate, economy and rank, that seemed to dictate the differences in foods and in eating customs.

The Chinese coolie or workman is said to be able to do more work on less food than any other human; his meals and his eating customs are the simplest possible. In the China of forty or fifty years ago the rich man — the important and successful man — despised physical exertion and was proud to be fat. Naturally he toyed with the most elaborate meals, served in the most elaborate manner that he could afford.

The chief Chinese cooking utensil is a shallow, round-bottomed frying pan called a *wak*. The fire may be of wood, charcoal, or of pressed coal dust; the wak also serves for cooking over modern gas or electricity. The second cookpot is an iron kettle for steaming. A little water is poured into the bottom of this, and with the support of two crossed chopsticks, two dishes can be steamed at the same time.

As in all these Eastern countries, much food of the snack variety is cooked and eaten right on the streets; sold from small street stands, in markets, and especially by wandering hawkers and peddlers, either women or men. The food is carried in a tray or basket swung from a long carrying pole on the shoulder, and may be anything from hot tea in a copper kettle to hot rice in covered containers. The system serves the same need as our vending machines which dispense cokes, hot coffee, popcorn and ice cream, or our drugstore counters and coffee shops.

The four basic Chinese foods are rice, soybeans, pork and chicken. Vegetables vary from district to district. In the more northern provinces, wheat, cooked the way we cook noodles, replaces the southern rice. The rice may be boiled, steamed, fried or made into a rice gruel, as well as rice water, rice wine, and a flour that is baked into noodles. Soybeans are the most popular vegetables; from these the cook makes bean paste and bean curd, and cooks bean sprouts and the spiced soya sauce which is used as a salty seasoning on many dishes. Pickled vegetables are popular, as they are in Japan, and bamboo shoots, garlic, cabbage, leeks, lotus roots, melons and onions are used much as we use most of them. "Black eggs" are a great delicacy. They are not really "hundred year old" eggs as they are sometimes called. They have been buried for some weeks or months to age them. They taste rather like truffles. Bird's-nest soup does not actually consist of nests

90

but it is thickened and slightly flavored by the gum which swallows make to attach their nests to cliffs.

The main meat dish is pork; fowl, duck and chicken come next in popularity, then beef, and of course every kind of fish and shellfish is used by the vast population that lives along the rivers and on the Chinese boats called *sampans* and *junks*. The Chinese, like the Japanese, eat few sweets, save at banquets, where they are served between the meat courses, not as a dessert. Among the well-to-do, baking is never done at home; baked foods are purchased at the town bakery, as in most countries where fuel is scarce and expensive.

This economy also applies to Chinese cooking, where nothing is ever wasted. Every drop of juice or gravy, every cabbage leaf, bit of celery or garlic, is saved for additional flavor to add to the rich and delicious soups. The rice crust, left in the cookpot, is allowed to dry, broken off into crisp pieces, and given to the children to chew on between meals. Milk and milk products are almost unknown, since the country is too crowded to allow grazing land for cattle, or even for goats; hence almost the only food the Chinese do not eat, and in fact do not like, is cheese. The children eat much as do the grown-ups, and they learn to handle the delicate chopsticks at an early age.

Though the main food of the Chinese peasant is rice, with the seasoning of soya sauce and now and then fish or a bit of pork for feast days, the great banquets of the rich in the days of the Empress were very grand indeed. These could last for hours and run into thirty courses. Again, they were not prepared in the household kitchen, but brought in from outside caterers.

Cooking on a charcoal stove on a *sampan* in Hong Kong Harbor.

Women and men did not as a rule eat together, though this custom is breaking down, as in all countries. Tables and chairs are used as we use them. The young folk wait for the elders to be seated, and for a nod of assent before taking their places. Each diner has his own bowl of rice, with his own chopsticks. Sipping hot tea between mouthfuls, he helps himself to meat and seasonings from the larger dishes in the center of the table. It is considered good manners to serve oneself only from the near side of this common dish.

After the meal, faces and hands are wiped with a clean cloth wrung out in hot water. At the family table, each leaves his seat to do this, but at a ceremonial banquet each guest is served with a hot cloth. One guest, having finished his meal, says to the others, "Eat at your leisure," which is his excuse to depart, if he wishes. Or he may leave his chopsticks across his emptied dish. The host then lifts them, saying, "I hope you walk in safety," as farewell and polite dismissal.

Two meals a day are customary; the first about eight or ten o'clock in the morning, though tea may be drunk earlier. For the poor, this early meal may be only a bowl of rice with a few vegetables and pickles. The same meal is repeated between four and six in the evening. But since the Chinese working day is a very long one, the laborer doing heavy work has as many as four or five short pauses during the day, for tea and a little rice.

Did you know that chop suey, so popular in America, and which we think of as a universal Chinese dish, is not Chinese at all, and originated here in the United States?

AFTERWORD

Now that we have learned about so many ways of eating and cooking around the world, it is interesting to stop and think about them.

It used to be believed that people who ate much meat became keen and strong and those who ate little meat would be lifeless and lacking in energy. We know now that this is not true. The Eskimo lives almost entirely on meat, the Chinese peasant may never taste meat throughout his whole life, yet both are physically enduring. We begin to see that what people live on depends on what grows in the country in which they live. This may depend largely on the climate, which will not allow the Lapp to grow vegetables, or the Indians of the High Andes to grow fruit. Sometimes too much of the land is occupied with farms and there is no grazing for animals, as in Japan, India and China, and this makes the people who live there almost vegetarians.

Methods of cooking depend a lot on what fuel can be found, so the Eskimo cooks with little lamps which use the grease and oils of fish and animals; the Arab often has to cook with dried camel dung; the Indians of Peru cook with twists of grass and a few twigs, and some must take their food to the village bakery, to save fuel.

Even table manners depend on the kind of food the country produces; some foods need knives for cutting, others need spoons, and some can be eaten tidily with the fingers.

What really is marvelous is the way in which people all over the earth have been able to adapt themselves to many different ways of living so as to make the best possible use of what their countries can grow for them.

AUTHOR'S NOTE

My collection of racial eating and cooking customs began on a visit to Lapland. It has since ranged over more than half the world, and through some twenty libraries. For six years it has been an exacting and rewarding pursuit.

Much of the data came from my own observation and notes; not always easy to obtain, for there is a tendency among quite intelligent natives of emerging countries to wish to erase the past and identify themselves only with what they feel is "progress." And, alas, this same progress may be seen only in terms of imported canned food, electric stoves and refrigerators.

Time was when there were none of these conveniences, so the accounts of early explorers seemed likely to furnish more valid data; from what food Marco Polo found in his long overland travels to a good recipe for cooking a castaway sailor in mid-Pacific, and the correct table manners when eating him.

The puzzle remains as to why so few travelers give any details about food or cooking. At times they almost starved and fell on their food with avidity. But what food? And how was it cooked and served? Peter Freuchen, T. E. Lawrence in his book, *The Seven Pillars of Wisdom,* and Wilfred Thesiger's *Arabian Sands* give more data than all the earlier trail breakers combined.

Such data as was available from such sources had to be eked out and brought up to date by studying anthropological reports, and by correspondence to various countries. Generous replies came from quite unexpected sources and much material became available. All this had to be sifted down, both in size and to suit the audience at which I aimed. This has naturally led to some generalization, but it was clearly impossible to cover the whole range of eating habits that varied from town to town, class to class, and religion to religion, of such vast areas as India, China and Africa.

Index

About the Author

ERICK BERRY has written over ninety books, most of them in collaboration with her husband Herbert Best. They cover a vast area of interest and travel as she has visited almost every country in Europe, spent six years in Nigeria, visited the Far East, and has a home in Jamaica.

Miss Berry is also an artist and has illustrated many books. She has provided for *Eating and Cooking Around the World* the black and white line drawings that begin each chapter.

96